C.C.

c.c.

Tyrone Williams

KRUPSKAYA · 2002

ACKNOWLEDGEMENTS

"Cold Calls" appeared in *Hambone* 15 Fall 2000
"I Am Not Proud To Be Black" appeared in *Callaloo* Vol. 22 No. 1
1999

Distributed by Small Press Distribution, Berkeley
800-869-7553
spdbooks.org

ISBN 1-928650-15-5

KRUPSKAYA
PO Box 420249
San Francisco, CA
94142-0249
krupskayabooks.com

CONTENTS

Called back.

Emily.

—May 1886

CALLING CARDS

"The CEO Of Comedy . . . 'Hiya, fellas' . . . Bob Hope, Inc:
U.S.N.S. Bob Hope, Spirit of Bob Hope, G.I. Bob, Hope
Memorial Bridge, Bob Hope High School, Bob Hope Street, the Bob Hope
Chrysler Detroit Golf Classic, Bob Hope Theatre, the Bob Hope
Ferry, the Bob Hope rose, the Bob Hope Steer, Bobby Hope, Ben Hope,

Bill Hope . . . Lester Hope . . . Leslie Townes Hope . . . " discombobulated
status qua "ad lib," qua "standup"—"or a cheap imitation"
of a machine—a formula for comedy—breadth, not depth—
a stripmall of one-liners and gags, a search engine called Yucks
.com. Man walks into a bar. Man walks his wife—leash, please. Man

walks into a telephone booth. Man, that hurts. Man stops and walks
into a telephone booth that has no telephone. It was
b.y.o.p. Man walks—cave drawing at 11:00 P.M.
S.—man walks, no, runs. Man walks into a phone booth as a man,
leaves as a superman. Hope dressed up in another caper.

Passed too slow—or too soon the waters unwalled.
    At either rate—
    passed over, under-

named—pacing leagues-deep in slow motion
    as the second
    woman on the moon—

"Albany's Rosa Parks"—arrested by a premature Chicago—
    post herself
    as Ola Mae

Quarterman-in-the-box long enough to pass
    as an heirloom
brought out for dusting and show on special occasions

    as her smile
passes by and circles back as a sprinkler—
    as a bird of prey

UPPER LEFT CORNER FOLDED "IN"

No seconds
          (acts or otherwise)—
                              firsts, thirds,
                 fourths, etc.,
enumerate
          bell curves:
                              15 minutes
                 (however long)
staged, tabled,
                 crown, cap,
                              careers (old hat,
                 however noble,
ignoble), stamping
                      "imagine" with
                              "for example,"
                 Toby/Topsy
posted a first
                 for the NYC
                              Ballet Company
                 (unattested
due to long-
          dead witnesses)
                              before the surname
                 gave out
short of the future,
                 leaving the tenor—
                              shorn of vehicle—
                 adrift post-first,
pre-third (Area
                 51,
                      for example)

                  until a chance—
disguised as grace—
              took sides
                        against the "equal
              opportunity"
of scales and torch,
           delivering a sentence
                        in the name
         of the third (limbo
of the nursing
         home) and the fourth
                     (rapture of kin)—
        twice saved
by Bell (this Arthur).

(Gots to be the backwardest craze I seen—
Do the stations in reverse—twelve steps
off the hook I got thirty years ago—
If I never see the inside from inside again—
Railroaded once too many—Don't close nothing now—
Open house 24/7 at the shotgun crib—
Every drawer pulled out—cabinet open—door cracked—
Look like rifled through—(rope-a-dope
fiend)—Important not to look like a fool—
Best study the juniors—'do's, threads, bull...
Ain't even 'bout "enabling," "disabling," "fabling"...
Ain't even... shit.. look like I'm up...)

Wussup. Go by Hayes Williams—
long for Say Hey the 2nd—
and I'm a black . . . I mean, African, American . . .

(1) Defull still, a man wakes up in the sixth (or to use the vulgar, "next") world, entangled in a leafless bush. (2) Thrashing about unsuccessfully, he does not see, not at first, the two figures a few meters away. (3) (a) names a boy face down in the sand, bawling inconsolably, next to him (b) names a kneeling man, pounding the ground repeatedly with his left hand, mumbling inaudibly save for the occasional ejaculation "glass" and "dark" . . . (4) Both the noise and sight of someone "thrashing" call and lift the man to his feet. Both the man on his feet and the man in the bush notice one another, almost simultaneously. (5) One walks toward the other, a metallic glint above, before, him. (6) As for the man embranched, it—inc. th frst ct—all comes back to him, to Yao-ting Sun, as the collective stooping over of namesakes, as grains per diem, as unabated heat, humidity. (7) As "then," the virtual appearance of a corner, a line, in brief, a change of life. (8) Or a tremulous modulation of fate. (9) Or a laying on of hands, largely onto shoulders and backs. (10) And whispers, rising and falling like hands. (11) And the abandonment of rapture insuring the family's fortune. (12) (Forsaken to a glorious future. (13) Even so, not his will (the "i" in kin always subordinate)). (14) How was he to know the hot chili sauce would anesthetize the wound and preserve the "three precious"? (15) What is consciousness that flees "phantom" and "actual" pain? (16) Repression and fainting (that is, the failure of total repression)? (17) Besides, the post-mortal roll-of-the-dice dubbed "marriage" and "children." (18) Besides, the oblivion of "normality." (19) All of that, what "really" happened, what did not, names history. (20) What would follow would yet be history, however defanged. (21) In short, the laying on of hands—across the bent ear, the insinuating tongue, of the emperor, to say nothing of the delicate fruits, the exotic meats, the exquisite silk. (22) In short, the reduction of history to the wave of a hand, the nod of a brow, the closing and opening of eyes. (23) Best of all, the family on its feet, at court. (24) Best of all, the

promise of "at last," the resutured, "full" man, called for the faith of the jar, the preservative, tempering the frustration of incontinence and thwarted passion. (25) As if the allure of the sixth dulled the ache of the fifth—world, as it is known. (26) As if the glint falling toward Yao-ting Sun might hack out the path to self knowledge: (27) Dupe. (28) Straight man. (29) And now as he recalls, for the last time in this (sixth) world, the shards of glass, the scattered remains, the chorus of screams and shouts, the falling peasants of his village, the pristine bayonets of the Red Guards, Yao-ting Sun laughs aloud, laughs alone, unjoined by the indifferent stars. (30)_____

CARDED

HAPPY FAULT

Who was it?
Was it for me,
you, or some
misnomer,
wrongly called
"Remember"-cum-comma
(something like that,
who could tell?),
tongue torn out,
favoring a hand?
Who will will
forth, something
leftover,
remarks of a body
of work, disparaged,
acclaimed?
Who recalls
what once dubbed
all the difference—
figure/ground—
no more so
than when both
appear as one?
Who beckons
from a fetal,
misshapened, delegged
future "i"?
Who will have
arrived save
for its limp,
glitch and catch,
belated, off-line,

staggered—or tapping—
off-stage, out-
side the flawed
wings? Who called
"Christians, Negroes,"
"Negroes, black
as Cain," but Cain,
nothing but Cain
with impunity?
Who else will call
and when, and if
no one, never,
who calls back?

"The First Time I Struck A Woman," by Sharon Olds, Donald Goines and Eve Kosofsky

A platitude is a hierarchy in the process of being veiled—not leveled.

FACE *QUA* FLASH CARD

"slimey looking"
"wears jacket on shoulders w/earring"
"no way . . . poor, poor, poor"
"avoids eye contact"   Wong
"smells"   Miguel

+   = Mohammed
                                              Swami
RK LP TP LR TC
                              Chang

State Department/Customs/INS Key:
"rich kid," "looks poor," "talks poor," "looks rough," "take care"

FLASH *QUA* FACE CARD

1. Or the reverse
2. _____people are_____
3. 186,000
4. Air Art—anything else is just a pair of dirty tennis shoes (net or not)
5. Market, mixed or centralized
6. This ouch ouches more than that ouch
7. 15, zed zed zed
8. The Constitution of the United States
9. (not to be politicized as labor)
10. "time"=the second law of thermodynamics means
11. Representin(g)
12. The Declaration of Independence
13. Life begins at_____
14. Film noir femme fatale—gender as a Gallic contagion
15. Nothing matters in the universe.
14. Character as a function of work
13. 14th Amendment
12. (not nil, naught, nada or "...and I'm all out of chewing gum")
11. "history"—the second law of thermodynamics means _____
10. Law
9. A mind is _____
8. Musical neighborhoods
7. 15th Amendment
6. 3.14
5. Traverse—don't
4. 1963
3. (urban promenades, eateries, galleries, thermidors, valets, and sufficient police presence)
2. Law above the law
1. save a single molecule of vinegar near the center of the Milky Way

"DISPELL'D"

after Walt Whitman's "Twilight"

Hereafter the so-called, remains no longer subject to the law of contraction and expansion intrinsic to dialectical materialism, no longer cohering in a "name" or a "body of work," no longer ideally irruptive ("anachronistic") or pandemic ("universal"), no longer—period,

however periodic, "Future/food . . . ," bread for the tongue, trail through the underbrush, almost as if the "man" taking in was not the "man" taken in, the backtracking pioneer and all that double/shuttle thinking . . .

>On June 4, 1892 buckturing@earthlink.com wrote:
Is the that-called this?

>On August 4, 1892 wltpplsd@aol.com wrote:
Can "loss" as a sensation or principle exist before the "idea" of life?

"If the 'old artificer' is not the end of artificial intelligence, does it make any sense to speak of 'end' or 'ends'?"

". . . a prejudice . . . Perhaps . . . "

P: When the mouth, tongue, and related apparatus evolve into absolute or near oblivion—hair, nails, etc. notwithstanding—will the name assume the form of a "sense" (assuming the aforementioned—plural or singular—survive the machinery of vocalization)—touch-just-so, see-such-and-such, etc.?

S: In any case, will the name always be the synonym of a suffix, always esque, ist, ian et al? In short, is the name possible before "outside" iteration? Does the answer—yes and no—point elsewhere?

No one, and I mean *no* one, calls me out of my name and gets away with it, you understand, you hear what I'm saying, you read me, I will *kill* me some motherfucker, don't you *ever* call me, I mean *never* unless I tell you to, you got that? Huh? HUH??!!

:I'm_____
:Hi. I'm_____
:A start, if only.
:And yet we thought it important enough to begin with introductions, aka names, as though they were shell-gifts, hollowed-out presents in which we might hear one another's blood.
:There exists a logic whereby we'd merely divulge information according to the complex parameters of human intimacy and then, and only then, give names.
:As statement, as if in a court of law, as if the moment of giving, there was assertion.
:Violence, then, still. And always, I suppose.
:Perhaps start again?
:Impossible. It's all out, there.

And

      and

         and/then:

                                   dislocation

                denames
                    (almost)

       —or, momentarily—

(that is, before

    post-i e

CALLED CARD

AFTER AFTER (lines toward adriftland)

All the same it
resembles oblivion,
and increasingly so,
afoul of light
refracted through the laws
of the prism house.
It howevers, tends,
thins, a gangrene
stmp from jump street.
Limp-fisted it
angles toward, slumps
against the ropes,
beseiged by a flurry
of theory-contracted
theorems, enforced disturbances,
defaced blueprints.
White red or black
green it steels
itself blues-hard—
brother v. brother,
sissified sisters.
So also.
       Too
isn't. It apes nothing,
remains out
of print. Only the great
I AM
      tenders, strikes through,
a call i're-
sponsibly

EL NEGRO

Here everyone—
            (in) or "in"—
                      is It—
          another name for "the"—
        or, decrossed, "-he"—
           delimbo-ed
     earthward,
first, at last, re-
              mains re
    stored re-
matriated
            to, by, the
motherland, her
         half-raised,
                  half-made
        fist, dethumbed
      down to *all fours*
                (do dodododo) lashed on,
    (da dadadada) reined in, in
order to show,
           later, place—
Africa—as if
          borne-reborne-
               across-The-Big-Sea
                       (aka
               pseudo-warp
        pseudo-woof
is be
     diminished return
             delimited statute
       uncorrected proof.

STUDY OF A NEGRO HEAD

This recalls a future "those_____ . . . "
future *then*, future unannounced
however called for
                        Indefinite
(forced march? ticker tape? Brownian?)
hand-made, -maiden
drawing of my face in 1528

Briefly, a sketch

                        An hoped-for
enlightened antelope for
                                prides (going after)
An afeared scatting Pops-cum-Gus Hello Dolly/Chase
the wee slaveholder with legs
                                (a runner never running
out of the frame)

                                A drawn out
in cahoots with arresting (Big, White, etc.) houses

Pewed—half-staffed swastikas—
[organ voluntary]
Gregorian crescendos,
belled by. Mini-stations
police the lamb fashioned out of gold.
[caroled organ] Adam
lay ybounden. Maiden, she makeless
[matchless], gentle. Better
Than the whole lot of them.
E'en so [organ responsory], quickly,
veni veni.

RIGHT OVER RIGHT

Yank—and yank—
and still the damned thing won't fit—
this green glove—
                    that brown hand.

Any vehicle with two tenors
jack-knifes. What it cannot carry over
is still freight—
                    unsecured futures:

Rainbow, gumbo, bowl of salad—
in short, collision cars—
spin-offs in
                    a cloud-chamber.

Don't breathe—Breathe through the snorkel
as they try to cut you out—
green wreckage—
                    (lockjaw-treasure).

If "I"-not-I offend seeing green
spear a pupil with a spit—
twist once—
                    yank.

COLD CALLS

¹ The spatial/temporal lacuna insures the possibility of temporary disruption—or permanent abortion—of service, insures only the probability of successful enunciation, its own passing over. Cf. Paul Laurence Dunbar as an example of such disruption, failure, breakdown: "My voice falls dead a foot from mine old lips/And but its ghost doth reach that vessel/passing, passing."¹

[2] God don't play that, so radio ratio—slippage: ebonics to tinkling the ivories, Eagle Nebula < M16, ice cream cones crowned with cherries, in short, EGGS, EGGS, EGGS . . . "In contrast, stars forming in more isolated circumstances presumably can continue to gather materials from surrounding gas clouds until their mature stellar dynamics halt their growth."[2]

[3] Foreign respondent—"How White American"—Amy Biehl—
"'Sister'"—chased across a street— "Died in a Township"—after her
car was stopped—"one settler"—by a crowd of youths—"one bullet"—
tripped—"I am not able to properly articulate any political ideology or
motivation for my conduct"—fell—"South Africa is free today because
of the bloodshed."[3]

Essay in a bottle cast out to sea, or placed in a jar on a hill in Tennessee, Penelope, weaving and unweaving, Scheherazade's thousand-plus deferments, time-lapsed Grecian Urn, bulk mailings, extensions of credit lines, free-market economies: manifold apocrypha: hope a project beyond approximate futures, Godot in which the thrown, not yet thrown back, esse.

[5] In the salad bowl of the museum, the Blonde Negress, a vigilant anachronism, deserts her post and joins her fellow patrons, a line refraining (in) the head she calls her body: "Lo, I am black but I am comely too." Among the periods, she attempts rememory: Is "but" conjunctive? Disjunctive? Her?[4]

[6] Not *de gustibus* but homegoing, via Heaven's Gate (< Hale-Bopp)—or another via: "Wherefore do we pray/Is not the God of the fathers dead?"[5] Or yet still a third via: "teeth or trees or lemons piled on a step."[6] Or yet still: two men sitting at a bar. One turns to the other: "Aren't you *the* Artie Shaw?" The other retorts: "No, I'm the other one."[7] Despite the end of identical actions at a distance (< Schrodinger's equation), pursuit converts us: ancestors of our hope, the via, the nectar.

⁷ from someone who, no longer there, abandoned headset swinging back and forth, fruit laced with strange, charm, top, and bottom—not vocabularized but ventriloquized—in an upright glass coffin rhyming with the "rough-hewn tribute in wood" to an anonymous African American rider, not "divinity alive in stone" aka "William Tecumseh Sherman at Fifth Ave. and 60th Street in Birmingham, Ala." An anti-Trojan, virus astride.⁸

[8] Inaudible howl, "foo seee like lee,"[9] the diving chrysalis[10]—hell with a little heaven in it[11]— and should it surface, should it find its way back home, should its first night back on earth not be its last

[9] Ambivalence of double cadence: an extra nail, or the anvil then the claw

[10] "Neither there nor there/ Almost here/ a little nearer to the stars/ strangers to the left and right/ pages turned, still to be turned,/ still there, never to be mine/ and here comes a smile/ which never arrives—/ 'Can I get you something?'/ 'Food/ For future years.'"[12]

[11] "All this in the hands of children, eyes already set/ on a land we never can visit—it isn't there yet—"[13]

[12] The "apron of leaves," the pieces of silver—what human, having embodied God as shame and guilt, would not be disappointed that only the same could disembody him?[14]

[13] The New Grammar: Neo-Babel: "Trucks, limousines and pickups . . . smashed to pieces." Crashing into a skyscraper, a Boeing jet "disgorged its sinful passengers," "bodies spilling across the road into 'The Peaceful View' cemetery"—paradigm of grammar and Babel—from which their spirits "floated upwards towards a glowing image of Jesus high in the clouds."[15]

[14] "A door ajar/ bereft of building/ remains unapproachable/ and mesmerizing." Tenor ISO vehicle. Rapture preferred but not essential. Will settle for oblique transport.

[15] you@notyetorever.com v .net v .org. v .edu v

END NOTES

1 Paul Laurence Dunbar, "Ships That Pass In The Night," *The Complete Poems of Paul Laurence Dunbar* (Hakim's Publications, 210 South 52nd Street, Philadelphia, PA 19139), p. 64.

2 *The New York Times*, 11/3/95 and 11/30/95, Science Sections.

3 *The New York Times*, 8/27/93 and 7/9/97.

4 Lewis Alexander, "The Dark Brother," *Caroling Dusk*, edited and with a foreword by Countee Cullen (Citadel Press, 1993; orig. Harpers & Brothers, 1927), p. 124.

5 W. E. B. DuBois, "A Litany Of Atlanta," *Caroling Dusk*, p. 27.

6 Amiri Baraka, "Black Art," *Transbluesency: Selected Poems 1961-1995*, edited by Paul Vangelisti (Marsilio Publishers, New York: 1995), p. 142.

7 *The New York Times*, 8/19/94.

8 Claude McKay, "Russian Cathedral," *Caroling Dusk*, p. 88; Judith Shea's "The Other Monument," as reported in *The New York Times*, 8/24/95.

9 Julia Tavalaro and Richard Tayson, *Look Up For Yes* (Kodansha International, 1997), p. 12.

10 Jean Dominique Bauby, *The Diving Bell And The Butterfly*, trans. by Jeremy Leggatt (Alfred A. Knopf, 1997).

11 George MacDonald: "There is no heaven with a little hell in it." Circa 1886.

12 William Wordsworth, "Tintern Abbey," in *English Romantic Writers*, edited by David Perkins (Harcourt Brace Jovanovich, Inc., 1967), p.210.

13 Miller Williams, "Of History and Hope," *The Ways We Touch* (University of Illinois Press, 1997).

14 Elaine Scarry, *The Body In Pain* (Oxford University Press, 1985), p. 360, footnote 23.

15 "The Coming Rapture," painting by an unknown artist, in Jeremy Marre and Hannah Charlton, *Beats Of The Heart: Popular Music Of The World* (Pantheon Books, 1985), p. 57.

WHO IS IT

I AM NOT PROUD TO BE BLACK

1.

Hope ends and thinking breaks out,
uncertain violence which is not despair—
or, if despair, sublime despair,
disfigured hope. The table, already broken,
gets cleared. Double consciousness gets swept aside
by polyentendres, duck-rabbits, wavicles.
Neither waving nor drowning, we tread water
like a page turning in a book.
We trace the arc of Icarus. The sky only
seems to fall—and then, only sideways
like a page turning in a book.
And in the larger arc of Daedalus, hope
settles in another country, ending
thought. We neither wave nor drown, we turn

2.

the page. We begin outside the book
but the text is everywhere we turn,
a finishing fable: cowboys "in the boat
of Ra" who "marvel at this curious thing":
hearsay circulates as he-said/she-said
to the put-down dubbed as he-said/he-said.
New commandments overdub the old ones.
Skin grows back over old bones:
Disfigured hope. The table, already broken,
dysfunctional, is finally institutionalized
as a work of art—or the black sheep
sold down the Jordan or the Nile,
another country cobbled out of continents,
extant and not: February, Juneteenth, Kwanzaa . . .

3.

"I wipe the spit from my face and read on."
We want more than this attenuation,
singularity, launch windows
so narrow, so fleeting, so hard to reach in time.
We need more than just a book called How
but the text is everywhere we turn:
Blue and his shopping cart of blueprints,
Trueblood in stitches—a howler—or a howl.
The face-cum-spit is not mollified
by inverted commas, an index of distance
shaped like a promise and a threat, a covenant,
a contract, on our lives. The principle flies
like a flag—or spit, returned with interest—
or we throw our hands in the air like we just

4.

don't care, nobodies or nations, the false dilemma.
We are neither, however concentrated
as teemings, trends or tendencies, bunched up
at—impaled upon—opposing horns
like shrunken heads or tails. The excluded middle
as "dispossession makes possession joy."
Reconstruction, acreage and mule, happy
days and endings: zero-sums: the median
strip: Begin Here to thumb rides
or jack cars. The two-way traffic—
shaped like a promise and a threat, a covenant—
waits for lights, not legs. It never strikes deals,
only pedestrians foolish enough to venture
forth. And yet, what choice but adventure?

5.

The lilies of the field? The birds? The median
strip: Begin Here to thumb rides?
I know, I know—the trap of the Missing Ingredient,
the Assumption of the Bloodied Bars. But prides
and flocks are never caged in zoos, obedient
in their calm, their rage. The slides and strides
of Skid and Strivers' Row enframe expedient
debts and assets, the obsequious calm of bromides.
We must almost come to terms and blows,
simulate in-flight, run in places.
To dart between the cars when traffic slows
invests an unsecured paper-chase.
Yet we cannot simply stand and wait
for deliverance. The shapeshifter debate

6.

concerns both strategies and goals. And both
depend on who we might, if we hold,
be as then, or such, or if. Suppose
we have, in fact, disappeared, or almost
so, absorbed unevenly—or woven
haphazardly—into the fold, which won't,
of course. For whom these variegated vectors,
these conflicting and overlapping methods?
And if this we is densities and clans,
storied skin, do we embody, en masse,
debts and assets, the obsequious calm of bromides?
Say nightmare? Yes, but say it backwards,
say it in a whisper over and over,
mute-nigh, narcotic nonsense, never

7.

to wake us. Falling deeper and deeper into
sleep, we could drift apart, into
unique dreams alike, dreams whose parents
look like us. What is not apparent
is the dream of nightmare, what we know
"before the voices wake us" and we know
light as day, the everyday, a dealer:
five-card stud or the five fingers,
it's all just bad hands, bad luck,
these conflicting and overlapping methods,
meterologies and weather reports,
"and" itself the means, obstacle and end,
"and" a better word for us than we,
or a better word for some of us.

8.

Case in point: Harriet Browne, stage
prop, brown dwarf, at Club Savannah,
glamorous, broke, despite the shim sham,
half break, break-a-leg, and sand
dance, "tripped and fell against a star."
She doesn't dream anymore, she sleep-
struts in ostrich feathers, twinkling sequins,
heels pounding, shoulders shaking, smoking
down stage, five-card stud
or the five fingers, grape or raisin, a showgirl
out of lock-step by the 1960's,
a relic amid the rattle of Charleston subways:
zero-sum crossover company stores
on rail for sharecroppers of all stripes.

9.

Take *The Labors Of Othello Simpson*,
how it was passed down from the Founding Fathers
under judgment: yoke of yore, prosthetic
prolepsis: Janus enters Hollywood
astride a pig, fleshing out the principle:
yes'em to death and destruction, suffer the slings
and arrows of *et tu* transfiguration:
celluloid and color commentary.
Such were the reparations for the future
slaughter, an epic in reverse order,
or an ordinary American story:
half break, break-a-leg, and sand

"what is this i said/some kind of goddam
joke i never joke/about money he said."

10.

Not called and not called back. Called
Abla Kator, called inside by "history.
its/hungrier than [she] thot"—called *trocosi*,
"slaves of the gods," the middle man's cut
come first blood. Called bushscaped goat,
unbeloved by Seth or Guinevere
Garcia, collaborators-*refusniks*, called,
uncalled for, slay-unslave their would-be Ablas,
would-be Kators. Called *Saterdagaandkind*,
test-tube Teun, Frankenstein Koan,
mixed-up, mixed-race, twins, untwinned to lord
or not: Jacob-Esau, Abel-Cain.
Such were the reparations for the future
daughter: daughters, errata *sous rature*.

11.

Or say the reverse: rear screen projection
of the wine-dark sea—or the Dark Continent
sans histoire—apparent *sui generis*—
thus the Dutchman's Burden—Black Pete—
Pullman porter more than Black Panther—
Good Cop—Chief assistant—roof-to-
hearth/cul-de-sac/acrobatic
sidekick slipping in and out of nooses.

What he isn't is like *Sinterklaas*:
Bad Cop The Boss booking kids
like his—Father Christmas, Santa Claus—
mixed-up, mixed-race, twins, untwinned to lord
it over Pops with hostile buy-out bids.

As for Pete—his *kieriegeld* affords

12.

him peace of mind. Is it complication
or compensation to see in making it
on and off the Long Island Rail Road
in one piece the spook who sits by
the door, a runaway virus in the program?
If Rosa Parks and Colin Ferguson were simply
doing their jobs, were they also simply
following orders? Who among us can—
and cannot—refuse the pink slip, slip
of the tongue? Give ourselves the slip? Perform
our own spinal cord operations?
Star and co-star in comic books, the hero-
sidekick slipping in and out of nooses:
public defender/defendant? The witnesses: "You"

13.

:Firestarter-smokejumper. Evasion
equals: A == A: Out of Egypt—
"But in what does this preservation
of African American culture consist? It can
hardly consist in anything more than eating
black-style food, listening to black-style music . . . "—
crawling back—"the oversocialized leftist
wants to integrate the black man
into the system and make him adopt its values"
on and off the Long Island Rail Road—
"the way of life of the black 'underclass'
they regard as a social disgrace"—
E > A:
Eyechart for eyes locked into

14.

one head *e pluribus*: Nation of Islam,
Republic of New Africa, NAACP,
Congressional Black Caucus, talented tenths,
capita, subject to the lowercases—
"the great burnings," uprisings, rebellions, disturbances—
subjected to *de*—Moore v. Dempsey, Plessy v.
Ferguson, Brown v. Board of Education,
Shaw v. Reno: "The New World, if misery
had/a voice would be a rifle cocking."
"What is tomorrow/that it cannot come/
today?" "Call it a blackman's ghost"
which "they regard as a social disgrace."
"To write a blues song/is to regiment riots"
rememory "love's austere and lonely offices."

15.

capita, subject to the lowercases—
eyechart for eyes locked into—
or compensation to see in making it—
sans histoire—apparent *sui generis*—
"slaves of the gods," the middleman's cut—
under judgment: yoke of yore, prosthetic—
out of lock-step by the 1960's—
light as day, the everyday, a dealer—
say nightmare? yes, but say it backwards—
simulate in-flight, run in places—
like shrunken heads or tails, the excluded middle—
singularity, launch windows—
as a work of art—or the black sheep—
or, if despair, sublime despair.

WORKS CITED

1. Charles Bernstein, *Content's Dream* (Sun & Moon, 1986)
Stevie Smith, "Not Waving But Drowning," *The Norton Anthology Of Modern Poetry*, eds. Ellmann and O'Clair (W.W. Norton & Company,1973)

2. Ishmael Reed, "I Am A Cowboy In The Boat of Ra," *The Norton Anthology of African American Literature*, eds. Gates and McKay (W.W. Norton & Company, 1997)
Countee Cullen, "Yet Do I Marvel," *Caroling Dusk*, ed. by Countee Cullen (Citadel Press Books, 1993)

3. Sigrid Nunez, as quoted in "The T.S. Eliot Problem" by Wendy Lesser, *The New York Times*, July 14, 1996
Ralph Ellison, *Invisible Man* (Vintage Books 1947)

4. Derek Walcott, "The Schooner *Flight*," *Derek Walcott: The Collected Poems: 1948-1984* (Farrar, Straus & Giroux, 1986)
Walcott, "Homage To W. H. Auden," *Every Shut Eye Ain't Asleep*, eds. Harper and Walton (Little, Brown and Company, 1994)

5. Paul Laurence Dunbar, "Sympathy," *The Complete Poems Of Paul Laurence Dunbar* (Hakim's Publications, Philadelphia PA)

6. Michael Harper, "Nightmare Begins Responsibility," *Every Shut Eye Ain't Asleep*

7. T.S. Eliot, "The Lovesong of J. Alfred Prufrock," *The Norton Anthology Of Modern Poetry*, eds. Ellmann and O'Clair (W.W. Norton, 1973)

8. Anne Spencer, "Innocence," *Caroling Dusk*, ed. by Countee Cullen (Citadel Press Books, 1993)

9. Ralph Dickey, "Father," *Every Shut Eye Ain't Asleep*

10. Ishmael Reed, "Dualism," *Every Shut Eye Ain't Asleep*

13. "FC," *The Unabomber Manifesto:Industrial Society And Its Future* (Berkeley, CA: Jolly Roger Press, 1996)

14. Michael Harper, "Homage To The New World," *Every Shut Eye Ain't Asleep*
Amiri Baraka, "Valery As Dictator," *Transbluescency: Selected Poems of Amiri Baraka/LeRoi Jones: 1961-1995*, ed. by Paul Vangelisti (Marsilio Publishers, New York, 1995)
Raymond Patterson, "Twenty-Six Ways Of Looking At A Blackman," *Every Shut Eye Ain't Asleep*
Etheridge Knight, "Haiku," *Every Shut Eye Ain't Asleep*
Toni Morrison, *Beloved* (Alfred Knopf, 1987)
Robert Hayden, "Those Winter Sundays," *Every Shut Eye Ain't Asleep*

and columns, articles and feature stories in *The New York Times*, 1992-1997

T A G

TAG

Addendum, p.s.,
by the way, almost forgot,
furthermoreover.

TAG

The theory beside
the flyhooked fly seduces
the short-range senses.

TAG

Silver chains of com-
mand identify remains
of etcetera.

TAG

The appetizer:
pre-quilt torn-up hand-me-downs.
The entree: ditto.

TAG

As in Scatterball,
Dodge and Colors, you—not I—
are It, It, legion.

TAG

NASA* et al crunch
colors, trade t-mail sans com,
net, org or edu.

TAG

Call me glove-slapped calf,
hacked arm, crosschecked back, clotheslined
windpipe, elbowed eye.

TAG

Files of little house-
and coffin-shaped immobiles:
half-mast flags big toes.

TAG

Letters and numbers
raised right on prison-pressed plates.
Vanity thy name.

TAG

Tipped-off gumshoe strings/
strung along. Close but not too
(net worth works gross play).

TAG

White sale. Will not last.
Everything marked down must go.
No refunds. Hurry.

T A G

Hung up by, on, or
both. Ordinary fruit. Boots
pulled up by, only.

TAG

The tie and jacket
vehicles given enough
velvet rope-a-dope.

TAG

A theory-proof lock
of hair wags the head. Tenses
fall out of their frames.

TAG

What was certain for
the most part parts uncertain
in the end, right?

*L.A.-based graffiti artists collectively known as No Art Survives After and, alternately, Nasty Artists Strikes [sp] Again (cf. *RapPages*, October 1998, 30-31).

ADDITIONAL NOTES

The section Calling Cards, after the Bob Hope parody, pays homage to Ola Mae Quaterman, a black civil rights fighter, Hayes Williams, one of the first prisoners whose conviction was overturned due to DNA technology, Arthur Bell, a former dancer with the New York City Ballet who was found homeless on the streets of New York City, and Yao-ting Sun, one of the last eunuchs to serve the last Chinese Emperor in the early part of the 20th century.

"Happy Fault" is dedicated to Phillis Wheatley. "Right Over Right" is inspired by Anna Akhmatova. "El Negro," more familiarly "El Negro of Banyoles," is the name given to the stuffed body of an African man displayed in Europe 1916-1917. In 1995 his remains were returned to Gabarone, Botswana. "Study of a Negro Head" is the title of an Albrecht Durer drawing.